First Facts®

The Strangest ANIMALS
IN THE WORLD

by Tammy Gagne

raintree
a Capstone company — publishers for children

Raintree is an imprint of Capstone Global Library Limited, a company incorporated in England and Wales having its registered office at 7 Pilgrim Street, London, EC4V 6LB – Registered company number: 6695582

www.raintree.co.uk
myorders@raintree.co.uk

Editorial Credits
Kathryn Clay, editor; Bobbie Nuytten, designer; Jo Miller, media researcher; Kathy McColley, production specialist

ISBN 978 1 4062 9311 1
18 17 16 15 14
10 9 8 7 6 5 4 3 2 1

British Library Cataloguing in Publication Data
A full catalogue record for this book is available from the British Library.

Photo Credits
Getty Images: Oxford Scientific/Gerard Soury, 13, 22, Photolibrary/Jeff Rotman, 5, 22; Minden Pictures: David Shale, 15, 22, Wil Meinderts, cover (bottom right) 21, 22; Newscom: blickwinkle/imago/imago stock & people, 7, 22, CMSP Biology, cover (bottom left), 9, 22, ZUMA Press/Liu Jian (Xinjiang), 17, 22; Shutterstock: almondd, 10, 22, Andrey Armyagov, cover (middle), Dudarev Mikhail, cover (top), 1, 11, 22, XIE CHENGXIN, 4, wormig, 22 (map); SuperStock: National Geographic/Tim Laman, 19, 22

Printed in China.
0914/CA21401516

Table of Contents

Japanese Spider Crab

Tiny bodies. Giant ears. Some animals are certainly strange. From a distance a Japanese spider crab looks like a giant sea spider. Its body is about 38 centimetres (15 inches) wide. But the spider crab's extra-long legs can span 3.7 metres (12 feet).

Fact: Japanese spider crabs live on the seafloor. Some may live to be 100 years old.

Star-nosed Mole

With its pointy nose, the star-nosed mole definitely looks different. But this odd appearance serves an important purpose. The 22 **tentacles** on the mole's nose can touch 12 objects each second. The tentacles help moles quickly identify if something is **prey** or not. Earthworms and insects that live in or on water make up a large part of the moles' diet.

Fact: Moles live under ground and are mostly blind. But they have the best sense of touch of any **mammal** in the world. They can tell if an item is food by touching it for less than a second.

tentacle long, arm-like body part some animals use to touch, grab or smell

prey animal hunted by another animal for food

mammal warm–blooded animal that breathes air; mammals have hair or fur; female mammals feed milk to their young

7

Pink Fairy Armadillo

A pink fairy armadillo might sound like a made-up animal. But it is indeed real. The smallest of all armadillos, it measures just 13 to 15 centimetres (5 to 6 inches) long. These unusual creatures hide in the sandy soil of Argentina and are rarely seen.

Fact: Most armadillos are completely covered by a brown outer shell. A pink fairy armadillo's pale pink shell only covers the top half of its body.

Fossa

When scientists discovered the fossa, they thought it was a rare cat. While its ears and body do look cat-like, its **muzzle** looks more like that of a dog. Related to the mongoose, the fossa is the largest **carnivore** on the African island of Madagascar.

muzzle animal's nose, mouth and jaws

carnivore animal that eats only meat

Irrawaddy Dolphin

Dolphins are not usually considered strange. But members of this river dolphin **species** look very different from the rest. Unlike other dolphins, Irrawaddy dolphins have no beak. They also do not whistle to one another the way other dolphins do. Instead, they **communicate** through clicks and buzzing sounds.

Fact: The Irrawaddy dolphin is an **endangered** species. Fewer than 100 of them live in Asia's Mekong River.

species group of animals with similar features

communicate share information, thoughts or feelings

endangered at risk of dying out

Dumbo Octopus

Named after the elephant cartoon character, the dumbo octopus has giant ear-like fins. Similar to the elephant character, dumbo octopuses flap their giant fins to move. These sea creatures are found as far as 4.8 kilometres (3 miles) under the ocean's surface. Few people have ever seen one up close.

Fact: Seventeen kinds of dumbo octopuses exist.

Gobi Jerboa

Look at another long-eared animal! The Gobi jerboa's ears are nearly as big as the rodent's body. A skilled jumper, this animal also has very long legs. Combine these features, and you have one of the oddest-looking animals in the world.

Fact: Gobi jerboas can survive a wide temperature range. In the summer the Gobi Desert can reach 40 degrees Celsius (104 degrees Fahrenheit). Winter temperatures can fall to -40 degrees Celsius (40 degrees Fahrenheit).

Superb Bird of Paradise

In many animal species, males are often more colourful than females. But the superb bird of paradise takes this quality to an extreme. The male can raise his feathers into a striking blue and black cape. He then performs a special hopping dance to get the attention of a female.

Fact: Female members of this species have black-brown feathers. The colours blend in with the surroundings to hide the birds from predators.

Sea Lamprey

A sea lamprey's jawless mouth makes it look like a creature from a scary film. Its round mouth holds rows and rows of teeth. Sea lampreys attach themselves to other fish and suck out their blood. Only one in seven fish that a sea lamprey attacks is likely to survive.

Fact: Sea lampreys once lived only in the ocean. Today, thousands have made their way into the Great Lakes of North America.

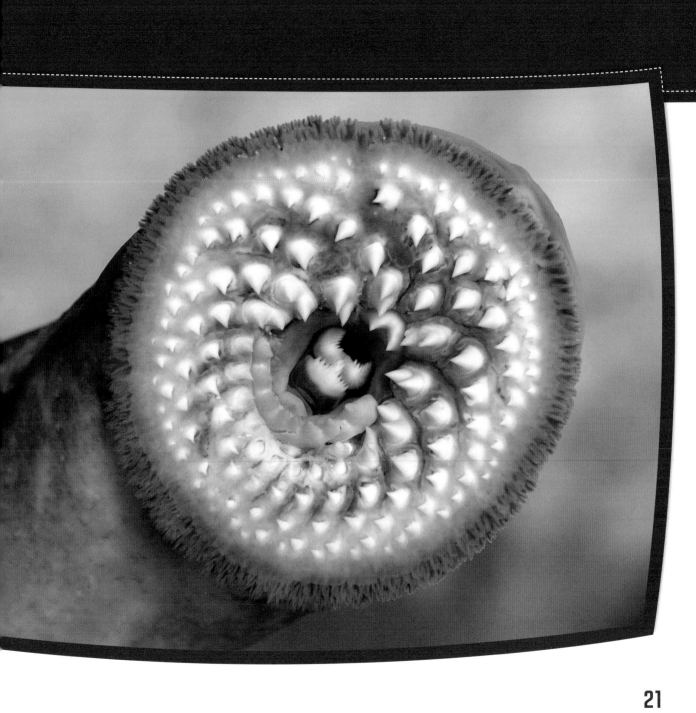

Habitat Map

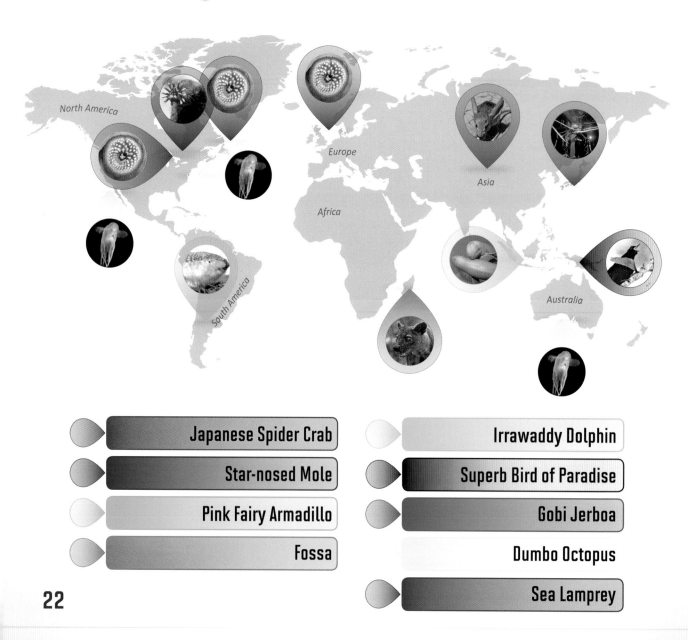

Japanese Spider Crab		Irrawaddy Dolphin	
Star-nosed Mole		Superb Bird of Paradise	
Pink Fairy Armadillo		Gobi Jerboa	
Fossa		Dumbo Octopus	
		Sea Lamprey	

Glossary

carnivore animal that eats only meat

communicate share information, thoughts or feelings

endangered at risk of dying out

mammal warm–blooded animal that breathes air; mammals have hair or fur; female mammals feed milk to their young

muzzle animal's nose, mouth and jaws

predator animal that hunts other animals for food

prey animal hunted by another animal for food

species group of animals with similar features

tentacle long, arm-like body part some animals use to touch, grab or smell

Comprehension Questions

1. Describe how male and female birds of paradise are different. Next, explain why they are different.

2. Look at the fact box on page 20. What may have caused sea lampreys to move into the Great Lakes?

Read More

First Encyclopedia of Animals, Paul Dowswell, (Usborne Publishing Ltd, 2011)

Interesting Invertebrates (Creatures of the Deep), Heidi Moore (Raintree, 2011)

The World's Weirdest Animals, Clare Hibbert (Arcturus Publishing Ltd, 2011)

Websites

http://gowild.wwf.org.uk
Learn about all types of animals, including information about their physical features, habitats and behaviours.

http://animals.sandiegozoo.org/animals/fossa
Learn about the fossa, including its habitat and behaviour. Find out how people are working to protect this unusual animal.

Index